Puffin Books
Paper World

A witch, a clown, a hedgehog, a princess or a magician –
these are just a few of the paper people and animals you
can make from ordinary paper, by cutting it into shapes
with scissors, and building and glueing the curved,
curled and bent shapes together into layers.

Following the clear, straightforward instructions, start
with a simple paper figure and gradually, as your
confidence and ability grow, you will find yourself
making the more elaborate pieces as easily as the simple
ones. The most rewarding thing is that once you have
mastered the basic techniques you can create more and
more complicated and exciting paper sculptures.

The methods described in this book are based on
techniques that have been in use for hundreds of years in
eastern Europe and elsewhere and which have been
simplified and modified over the years.

Clive Manning first became interested in paper
sculpture when he was eight years old and has studied
the techniques ever since. His largest piece to date is the
'paper palace' which was on show at the 1975 Puffin
Birthday Exhibition.

Paper World is a supremely straightforward and
rewarding introduction to the art of paper sculpture which
will set many other people off on an explorative trail.

Clive Manning

PAPER WORLD

Puffin Books

Puffin Books
Penguin Books Ltd,
Harmondsworth, Middlesex, England
Penguin Books Inc.,
7110 Ambassador Road, Baltimore, Maryland 21207, U.S.A.
Penguin Books Australia Ltd,
Ringwood, Victoria, Australia
Penguin Books Canada Ltd,
41 Steelcase Road West, Markham, Ontario, Canada
Penguin Books (N.Z.) Ltd,
182–190 Wairau Road, Auckland 10, New Zealand

First published 1976
Text and Illustrations copyright © Clive Manning, 1976

Made and printed in Great Britain by
Richard Clay (The Chaucer Press) Ltd,
Bungay, Suffolk
Set in Monotype Ehrhardt

Contents

List of Plates

(between pp. 32–33)

Chapter 1

Paper sculpture is the art of making objects out of ordinary paper, by cutting the paper into shapes with scissors, and then building the shapes together by sticking them with glue. The paper is curved, curled and bent into different shapes as it is glued, and the finished object can look quite elaborate, just by using layers of different shapes, one over the other.

The ways of making the things described in this book are based on methods which have been in use for hundreds of years, particularly in eastern European countries where they make magnificent festive decorations.

By tradition, such paper sculptures are made with white paper, which means that the shaping of the paper is the most important thing, and nothing else needs to be added.

If you are painting or drawing, you can make the outlines of objects clear by a change in tone or colour, but in paper sculpture the work is already done 'in relief' and needs nothing but its own shape – rather like carving a statue, where shape is important and colour not necessary.

However, coloured paper can help bring a paper-sculpture subject to life. This means that the sculpture does not rely so much on the shapes used, but more on the colour of its different sections, so less precision is needed with coloured work than with white.

One of the best types of paper to use is *coloured cartridge –*

the basic coloured card sold in any art shop. It isn't essential to use cartridge; *sugar paper* will do, and is also sold in different colours. Even a thicker writing paper can be used if you should want to do something that is all white.

Don't use anything too flimsy, as it is more difficult to work with. On the other hand, if you use a paper that is too stiff and cardlike, it will not bend into shapes very well, especially into the smaller curved shapes you will come across later.

The gummed paper sold in some shops is in the 'flimsy' category. It is useful for laying colours on to other, stronger, pieces of paper, but unsuitable for use on its own.

Another reason for avoiding lightweight papers (such as newsprint, brown paper, etc.) is that when you begin to make larger pieces of paper sculpture, you will find it difficult to make them stand up on their own, and they will be so fragile that they have to be handled very carefully. A cartridge-paper sculpture, however, can be handled reasonably roughly, in spite of its fragile appearance.

The basis of most paper sculpture is a cylinder, and if you use medium-weight paper (card) you will need a fairly strong adhesive. If you try to make a cylinder using a paste glue, the paper is likely to become wet without being very sticky, and your cylinder shape will spring open again.

Quick-drying adhesives are best for the job, unless you have endless patience and can spend hours holding the edges of your cylinder while the glue dries!

Clear adhesives are best for use with paper sculpture. These adhesives may appear to be the most expensive, but a little goes a long way and it is false economy to buy a cheaper glue, as you will use a lot more of it and need a lot more patience.

The only other tool which you will need is a pair of scissors.

Some books on paper sculpture suggest that you use a sharp knife, but this is not necessary.

Make sure that your scissors are sharp. Blunt scissors will only cause 'furry' cutting lines, and spoil the look of the finished object.

Pointed blades on your scissors are also useful, because with them you can cut holes into the middle of a piece of paper. With round-ended scissors, paper is best cut into from the edge; and this means that you can't do some of the more interesting pieces.

Chapter 2

When you work with a medium-weight paper, you will find that when you try making a cylinder it is very slightly easier to bend the paper one way than the other.

If you cut a small square (about 10 cm. [4 in.]), you might be able to see a slight natural curve in the card. The way this curve lies must be considered when you make your cylinders.

Paper has a grain rather like the grain in a piece of wood. Although you can often see it running across some of the heavier cards, it is invisible in many, and the only way to find out which way it runs is to try making your piece of paper into a tight cylinder.

Take the small square you have cut, and roll this into a tight tube. If the sides of the tube form a nice, rounded shape, which is quite smooth, then you have made the tube correctly – that is, with the grain running from top to bottom of the shape (figure 1).

If your tube seems to have a series of uneven creases running round the edge, then you are trying to make your tube curve *against* the grain (figure 2).

Even if you made a perfect cylinder the first time, it is worth bending your square card in the other direction too, just to see what happens.

It is particularly important to know which way the grain

lies in your paper when you want to make some of the smaller curves, such as curled hair.

It is a good idea to mark the whole large sheet of card in one corner with an arrow, to remind yourself which way the grain is running, so that any piece you cut can be made to curve the right way first time.

Test each colour you are using separately, for although the grain *usually* runs along the longest edge of a sheet of card (which means that it should be rolled up longways), this is

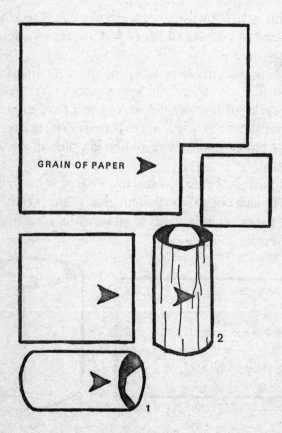

GRAIN OF PAPER

by no means the rule. Different sheets of card can have the grain running in different directions.

Having made your marks to remind you of the direction of the grain, you are now all set to make a proper cylinder. Simply cut out a rectangle whose length is almost twice its height. As you progress with the different methods in this book, you will get to know exactly how large this rectangle should be to suit your own work.

As a guide, try working with one 8 cm. by 15 cm. (3 in. by 6 in.), or slightly bigger (figure 3).

Glue this *lightly* down one edge, and curve your rectangle so that this edge lies *over* the other edge. Glue *inwards*, for neatness (figure 4).

Place your thumbs along the join, and your index (first) fingers outside the tube. This way, you can make sure that the glue sticks all the way down. You will have to hold the cylinder for about thirty seconds to make sure it sticks properly; this is probably the longest adhesion time in the whole construction.

If you have succeeded in making a satisfactory cylinder, there isn't much else to worry about. The cylinder is the basic shape in paper sculpture, either straight, or smaller at one end (tapered).

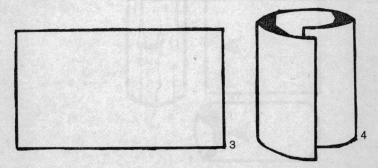

3

4

It is surprising how strong a cylinder can become when other pieces are glued to it.

The first photograph (plate 1a) shows a fish shape made out of a series of cylinders, the first group stuck by their sides to a backing board, then the others stuck to each other *and* the first (sideways) ones. This fish looks as if it is very fragile, but it is really quite strong. Each piece gets stronger as another piece is stuck to it.

Try making up a design of your own using only cylinders; such as a bird, or a butterfly.

Don't try to attach cylinders to the backing board by putting glue round the rim. This not only looks messy but is a fairly useless way of sticking things, as there isn't much of the cylinder to stick against the board.

Do your design as described for the fish, first gluing your cylinder down one side and laying it on its back and then building your design out from the centre.

Chapter 3

Having learned how to make cylinders, the next steps involve adding on to and cutting away from this shape to make it into a face. The three characteristics of a face which should be done in order are: (1) Eyes; (2) Nose; (3) Mouth.

The eyes come first so that you can make sure which side of your cylinder is the front (keep the join to the back).

The nose is next so that you can tell where the mouth should come. If you try to put the mouth on before the nose, you might get into difficulties – like finding that the nose is too short. It's always better to make the nose too long than too short, because it's easier to cut some off than to disguise where you joined some on!

As there is more than one method of making the eyes, nose and mouth shapes, I will tell you both the *Simple* (easy) way of doing them and the *Complex* (difficult) method.

Eyes

SIMPLE METHOD

Cut out two circular pieces of card, and with a small dab of glue stick these on to the cylinder (figure 5). You might find it easier to fold a piece of paper double, and then you can cut out both the eye shapes at once. This makes sure that both pieces end up the same shape and size.

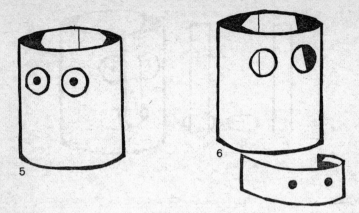

If you find a circle a difficult shape to cut, draw round a coin first, but make this circle quite large. It doesn't matter if the eye stands out a bit from the cylinder. This can be disguised in later stages. Whilst these circles are drying, you could be cutting out two smaller pieces, in a darker colour, to add to the eye centres as pupils.

COMPLEX METHOD

With pointed scissors, cut two equal circles into the cylinder. These circles should be in about the same position as the eyes would be if the simple method were used. They should also be about the same size.

Next, cut a strip of white paper, about three quarters of the perimeter of your cylinder, with the grain running from top to bottom of the shortest edge; and glue the ends of this strip lightly (figure 6).

Insert the strip inside the cylinder, so that it fills in the eye-holes you have cut. Keep this strip a bit farther back than the wall of the cylinder. Hold it in place while the glue dries.

Again, in a darker colour, place the pupils of the eyes.

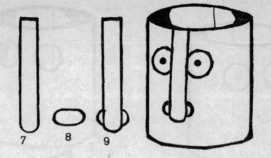

Nose

SIMPLE METHOD

Cut a strip of paper (figure 7), and cut one end so that it is rounded off.

Put a dab of glue on the opposite, square, end (the top of the nose strip), and stick this strip down between the eyes. The nose strip should keep its flatness, and stand out a little in relief of the cylinder.

Take another smaller piece, the same width as the nose strip, and round off both ends (figure 8).

Glue this piece behind the bottom of the nose, just above the rounded part. This makes 'nostrils' and finishes off the nose shape (figure 9).

COMPLEX METHOD

If you use the complex method, you can provide the face with a nose, a forehead and eyebrows at the same time. Take a piece of card which is the same height but not as wide as your cylinder, and with the grain running in the same direction. Study figures 10, 11, 12 and 13.

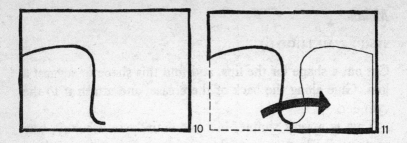

First cut the shape in figure 10 from the side of the card, and curve round to make the shape of an eyebrow. Carry on cutting down to make one side of the nose, but stop cutting at the centre of the rounded-off base of the nose shape.

Fold over the piece of card you are *not* going to use to the opposite edge, as in figure 11, so that the fold comes under the centre of the rounded section. This piece you have just folded over now acts as a template to follow, so that you can match the second side of the nose to the first and make sure that it comes out the same shape.

The lips and mouth can also be attached either by sticking on or insertion.

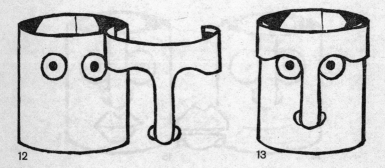

Mouth

SIMPLE METHOD (i)

Cut out a shape for the lips, and fold this shape to suggest a join. Glue along the back of the crease, and attach it to the cylinder.

This is a very simple, but not entirely satisfactory, way of doing the lips, because there is not enough paper touching the cylinder to form a strong join, unless you use *tabs* (see Chapter 5).

SIMPLE METHOD (ii)

Cut out two shapes separately, one for the top lip and one for the bottom lip. Add a little extra to the depth of each piece (figure 14).

Next, cut a slot in your cylinder to put the lips into. Make this slot low enough to allow for the upper lip; it should also be a little wider than the lip shapes themselves.

Fold over the extra you have allowed on the *bottom* lip only. Glue this on the underside. Then it can be 'hung' from the slot, and stuck on the inside of the cylinder. Don't put glue on the part that is going to show.

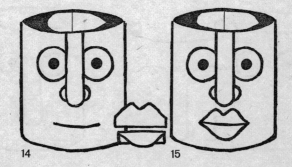

14   15

When the lower lip is dry, glue the extra bit of card on the upper lip, on the side facing. Insert this strip, *without* folding, into the same slot. Don't put on too much glue and don't let it get high enough to show after the lip is in place. All glue should be concealed when the face is finished (figure 15).

COMPLEX METHOD

Cut a square shape into the bottom of the cylinder (figure 16). The width of this square should be about the same as the distance between the pupils of the eyes.

Then cut out a rectangle at least 4 cm. ($1\frac{1}{2}$ in.) larger all the way round than the square you have just cut away from the cylinder. Curve the lower edge of this square into a chin shape. This can be pointed, rounded, or square with rounded corners.

Experiment with different chin shapes. The chin is one of the features which can change a face completely.

Glue the top two corners of the chin shape on the side facing. Curve it so that its bend is slightly sharper than that of the cylinder. Stick it in place in the cut-out square.

You can place it at an angle as well, so that the chin sticks out a bit from the straight front of the face.

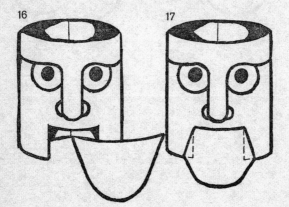

16   17

As this piece has only been glued at the top you can trim the sides of the square cut into the cylinder into curves so that the edges of the square are made to meet up with the edges of the chin shape. The dotted line in figure 17 shows the sections cut away in doing this.

All these ideas can be used in a mix-and-match way. The lips described in the simple methods can be used by attaching these to the square and to the top of the chin section, before assembly (figure 18).

Alternatively, before inserting the chin shape, a curve can be cut into the top edge (figure 19) to suggest an open mouth.

18

19

Chapter 4

Curling paper for hair is a relatively long job, but becomes more exciting as the layers are added and you can begin to see the face taking on a personality.

The most effective and easy method of making hair is to curl the paper with your fingers.

Finger Curls

Take a rectangle of paper, and cut strips into it; but only after making sure that the grain of the paper is running *across* the strips, so that they can be curled up without buckling. Leave these strips attached together at one end of your rectangle (figure 20).

To make these strips into tight curls, it is easier to weaken the strip at one end by folding it into a small square, then folding this square in half, and then folding the small piece left in half. This will give you three folds at the end of your strip, and if you pinch and roll this at the same time, it will roll round and under itself.

It is worth trying this a few times if you find it difficult, because, once you have mastered it, this method becomes the easiest way to start a curl. You might also find that it helps stop the paper slipping when you pinch it, if you lick your fingers lightly before starting the roll.

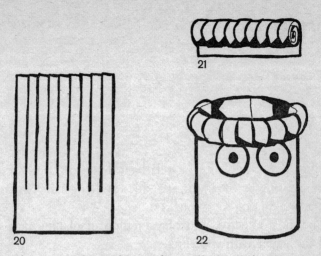

20 21 22

Keeping your fingertips moist, roll the strip down to its join.

When you let go, it will unroll only very slightly, and you will be left with the tightest curl you can get with paper, and this process can be repeated all the way along the strip (figure 21).

This first strip of curls can then be placed *inside* the cylinder, with the curls over the edge (figure 22). This hides the edge of the cylinder, and helps give it a rounder shape.

The second strip of curls can be attached to the back of the first strip, and can be placed slightly higher; and so on.

If you go all round the inside of the cylinder, you can gradually reach the middle in this way.

Try putting some of the later strips on the other way round, pointing into the middle. This way, you will reach the centre more easily.

The advantage in fingercurling is that the curls can be controlled. The curling process can be stopped halfway along a strip, and left. This means that strips of curls can be made into a V-shape or a rounded shape. If either of these is repeated for more than one layer, the effect becomes confused, and so a very effective hairstyle can be made by fixing curls all over the back and sides of the cylinder, on the outsides.

Scissor Curls

This method is one of the most widely known ways of curling paper, but has the disadvantage of not being as controllable as fingercurling.

First, cut a rectangle into strips, as described for finger curls.

Take your scissors, open them and place one strip between your thumb on one side and the blade on the other. Pull the paper between your thumb and the blade as you grip it, and it will develop either a curve or a curl, depending on the weight of the paper you have chosen for this. Repeat this along your row of strips.

Scissor curls are never as tight as finger curls, and cannot be controlled in the same way; but this is the best way to get a long, casual look to the hair. It is more effective to use a darker coloured paper with this method.

Ringlets

Two extra items are necessary for making ringlets. The first is a round piece of wood (a large knitting needle or a round pencil will do). The second is a hair-dryer or a fan-heater. Have some water available, as well.

First, cut a long, single strip of paper, with the grain running across it. Pull this quickly under a tap, or through a bowl of water, squeezing it as it passes through, to make sure it doesn't get too wet; if it does, the paper will fall apart. Wind this damp

25

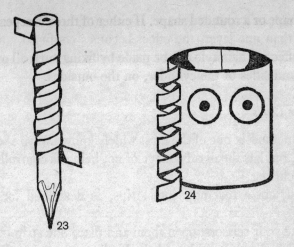

strip round and down your pencil (figure 23). Hold the last wind down and tuck the first one under itself so the strip doesn't unravel. Dry the wound strip well with the hair-dryer.

When it is half dry you could loosen your grip a little, so that the coil unwinds a bit and the warm air can get to the inside as well. Later the pencil can be removed, and the ends of the coil held in place, while the drying-off is completed.

This ringlet, when dry, will stay curled like a spring; and it can be used with others down the side of a face, or, instead of finger curls, wound round to fill in the top of the cylinder, with each strip of curls attached to another by the sides. (figure 24).

Curved Strips

With this method, the first step is the same as finger or scissor curls, except that when you make your comb of strips they are cut longer, and curved over in cutting, to one side (figure 25).

26

Inside the cylinder, stick a strip of paper, rounded from the front to the back of the head.

The hair sections can be attached first to the cylinder; but when you do this, stick them round the inside of the top, sticking up out of the head. Then the strips can be curved over one or two at a time, and stuck to the sides of the cylinder in overlapping shapes (figure 26).

The hair can then be built up until the strips look fairly thick, and then more strips stuck to the piece across the cylinder (figure 27). These can then be 'woven' into the style.

This method may need some practice before the best curves for hairstyles are found. The method is illustrated in plate 2b.

The strip laid across the cylinder can also be used to help fill in the cylinder with finger curls, scissor curls and ringlets.

If you don't want to fill your cylinder with curls, you could finish it more easily with a hat. If you decide to put a hat on your cylinder, attach the hair afterwards.

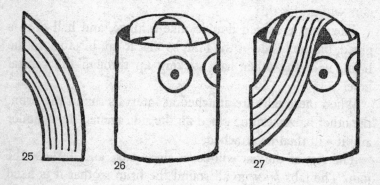

25 26 27

Chapter 5

To make a 'boater' hat, begin by making the brim. Put the head cylinder upside-down on a piece of card, draw round it and cut out the middle.

This cut-out hole has to be in the centre of a larger round shape, so cut the card again, this time about 2 cm. (1 in.) outside your first cutting line. This is the brim of the hat, and can be slipped over the top of the cylinder until it is the required height above the eyes. To make this shape stay put, you will have to fix it with a few *tabs* (figure 28).

These tabs are made from small strips of paper – your off-cuts will do for this.

The strip is folded double, like a hinge, and half of it is glued, on the inside of the fold, so that it can be stuck to the brim, with the other half sticking up through the central hole.

When these tabs are attached at intervals round the brim, the other halves can be glued on the side against the cylinder and it will then be attached.

The rest of the hat will cover these tabs, and disguise the join. The tabs *must* go all round the brim so that it is fixed firmly in place.

The rest of the hat is made from a piece of card the same width as your first cylinder, though only as high as you want your hat to be.

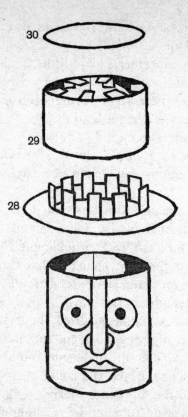

The back seam of this piece can be glued as you attach it, to ensure a snug fit. It is important that it is firmly attached to the basic cylinder, by gluing round the inside. This is also a reason for leaving a little extra height on the head section (figure 29).

This extra cylinder could, if you like, be made long enough to be a top hat, instead of a boater. If you are making a lady's hat, you could add some character by putting some cut-out flower shapes on the brim. Try cutting out two or three flower shapes of the same size, and then fixing them to each other, so that you have layers of petals. You could also add a hatband of a different colour.

It is by bringing together a lot of little details like this that you can end up with a very ornate-looking paper sculpture.

It isn't absolutely necessary to fill in the top of your cylinder, as paper sculptures can be made so that they are viewed only from the front; but if you feel that it needs to be filled in, use the circle you first cut from the centre of the brim. If you have cut this with an untidy edge, cut a new circle the same size (figure 30).

This has to be attached with tabs as well, but this time they are arranged in a different way. Glue only half the strip you are going to use for a tab, without folding it. Stick this to the inside of the top of the hat cylinder, so that it sticks up (this is similar to sticking on straight strips for hair). Place a number of tabs round the cylinder in this way.

When the glue has completely dried, these tabs can be bent towards the centre of the cylinder, and the circle you have cut out can then be glued on the underside, round the edge.

Place the circle on the tabs, and hold it there while the glue dries. If you find the top is not sticking well, you could try pressing the tabs against the top by reaching up through the whole cylinder with your closed scissors, or a long paint brush, to put a little pressure behind each tab separately.

Having used and explored the cylinder shape, we can now move on to a second popular shape in paper sculpture – the cone.

The cone makes a hat for a magician, a witch or even a Chinaman.

One end of a cone is similar to the end of a cylinder, whilst the other is a sharp point.

A cone uses a comparatively large piece of paper, as it involves using a circle for the basic outline, where the cylinder uses a rectangle.

The cone is another shape which you may need to experiment with, as the size of your circle governs the height of your cone.

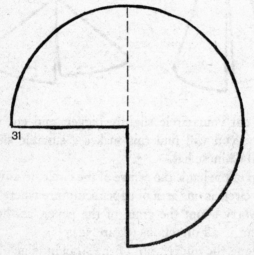

31

The *height* of your cone depends on the *radius* of the circle.

The outside measurement of the circle (the circumference) is the part that will have to be long enough to fit on top of the cylinder.

If you cut a piece of string to the same circumference as the top of your cylinder, adding a little extra for the glued overlap, you will be able to curve this round objects until you find something of the size you are looking for.

If you look at figure 31, you will see that some of the circle has to be cut away to make a very pointed cone – only half the circle is used for the witch's hat – so your string will have to be long enough to go along the curved edge you have left, *after* cutting a section away.

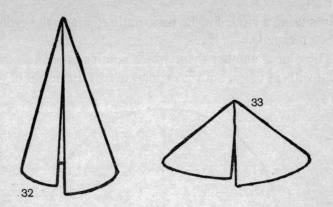

32

33

If you cut your circle slightly bigger, and cut very little of it away, you will find this makes a suitable shape for a traditional Chinese hat.

The top of the hat is the centre of the circle, in any instance. Cutting a circle is one area of paper sculpture where you don't have to worry about the grain of the paper, as the piece of card is bent in all directions (figure 32).

Glue along the underneath of the straight edge on one side (or along *half* the straight width of the circle), and overlap the two straight edges to stick.

Even at this stage, the amount of overlap can vary the degree of point to your cone. Be careful not to overlap too much, or you will find that your cone no longer fits your cylinder properly.

For the Chinese hat, the slope should be very gentle (figure 33), and can be attached with tabs to the head, in either of the ways described earlier.

If you are making a witch or a wizard, you might like to give it some character with the addition of long, flowing hair.

The easiest way of doing this is to fix the hair to the hat, to fall from the inside. Then you can still fix the hat to the cylin-

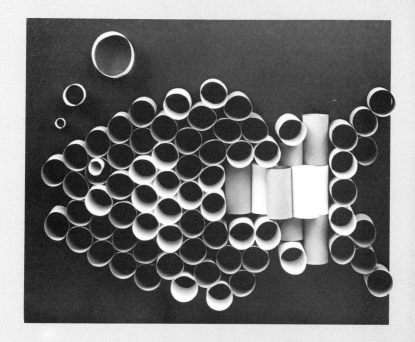

1a. The Fish Shape

This is built up of cylinders, each glued to the next, as described in Chapter 2.

1b.

The first face is made by use of the complex nose and eye methods (Chapter 3). The cheek shapes are made by using the left-over shape from cutting out the nose. The face to the right is the same, but finished with strip hair.

The face below is made by the simple methods described. Alongside it is the same face, finished off with finger curls.

2a. Bunch of Cones

These have been arranged in regular shapes to form a pattern.

2b. The Three Kings

The centre figure was made first, and a cross-piece was added to his shoulders. This supports the two outside figures, and ensures that they all end up the same height.

2c. The Jester

His thin legs are possible because his body has been stuck to the backing board, so he is not actually resting on them. Here, as in the Magician and the Kings, I used repeated cylinders.

3. The Magician

Here is one character who has a conical
hat. His hair is stuck to the hat, and
the hat stuck to the head. The rabbit
was made separately, and put in his
sleeve; and the bird was also made
separately, and stuck to his hat.

4. The Princess

Her dress uses repeated cylinders, and the join at the waist is made less obvious by overlaying strips, as described in Chapter 7. The hair is made of very fine ringlet curls, stuck one to the other.

5. The Bishop

Cylinders are used again to shape the Bishop's robe, and the join at the waist is disguised by his stole and medallion. The ribbons of his mitre are actually stuck flat onto the backing board.

6a. Hedgehog

The hedgehog is shown in the different stages of construction and described fully in Chapter 9. With legs and a coat of ringlet curls added, this shape can become a sheep, or, in pink, with no coat, but a flat nose and curly tail, it becomes a pig.

6b. The Sheep and the Pig.

7a. White on Black

All the shapes shown here have been cut out symmetrically, with a fold down the centre, like the cat shown in figure 58.

7b. Alice and the Duchess

These are a combination of flat pieces, used for the farthest legs of each character, and laid-on paper sections for the faces; I also used 'squashed' cylinder shapes, described in Chapter 10.

8a. The King and Queen

Here there are many examples of the curved strip. The King's fur is made of crumpled grey tissue. The Queen's long face gives her a stern look, while the King's crown slipping over his eyes makes him look confused.

8b. Party Pieces

These simple little figures use most of the techniques in this book.

der with tabs (figure 34) and the hair doesn't get in the way at all, as it tends to be the same shape as the cone.

Tabs are the best way of fixing any cone to a cylinder, as the two shapes do not fall naturally together.

You can glue these tabs and then reach into the cylinder with some long object to help secure them, as if you were putting the top circle on a hat.

A witch's hat also needs a rim round it. This can be done exactly the same way as making a rim for the boater.

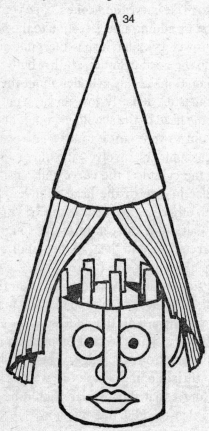

34

Chapter 6

So far, we have learned how to make a cylinder, how to use tabs and how to make curves and cones. Now you can build up your figure, first by adding a neck section to the head cylinder.

Make a narrower cylinder, using the same methods, and stick this inside the head cylinder, so that both seams are together. You should make this cylinder about the same height as the head, but stick it fairly low down. You must have a neck to attach the head to the shoulders, but it does not always have to show, unless you want it to.

Making the shoulders involves the three techniques we have learned: the cylinder, the curve and tabs. First, take a rectangle similar in size to the head cylinder, but with the grain going the other way, so that it can be curved along its shortest side. Cut from the centre of one long side into the middle of the rectangle, and then, in the middle, cut a circle a little bigger than the neck size (figure 35).

If you need to use the neck as a guide to do this, and have drawn round it, turn the card over so that any pencil lines still showing after cutting are on the underside.

The next step is to join the card by overlapping the edges made by cutting in from the edge. This overlapping gives the shoulders their sloping shape, as well as securing the paper. Don't forget that this overlap should be glued on the underneath, so that the glue doesn't show.

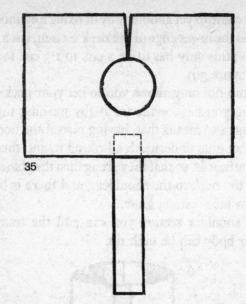

35

The shoulder shape needs only one tab; but this, unlike those used before, should be long and fairly broad. This is fixed opposite the overlap, and to the underside (see figure 35).

It is important to allow the glue time to dry on this piece before making the next move.

When it is dry, bend the rectangle over, tab towards overlap, so that the curve is roughly the same as in the head cylinder. Bend the tab so that it lies straight across the gap between the straight edges (this is not a full cylinder, but a half cylinder), and bend up the tab at the other end, so that it hooks the back at the correct width.

This means that it becomes a 'double' tab – two tabs in one – a straight strip underneath your curve, with two folded-up ends, one stuck to the underneath front edge, and one which can then be stuck either over or under the back overlapped edge.

Now we come to yet another way of fixing a cylinder by tabs.

All round the lower edge of the neck section, cut a 'comb' of short strips; this only has to be 1 cm. to 1·5 cm. (about ¾ in.) in depth (figure 36).

This comb not only allows you to get your neck shape *into* the opening you have made for it (by pushing the strips in slightly), but also means that, having placed the neck into the hole, you can glue underneath all round it, and then bend all the strips outwards, so that they are against the glue (figure 36). This fixes the neck to the shoulders, and there is little possibility of the tabs coming loose.

To this shoulder section you can add the framework on which your body can be built up.

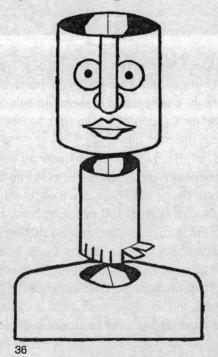

36

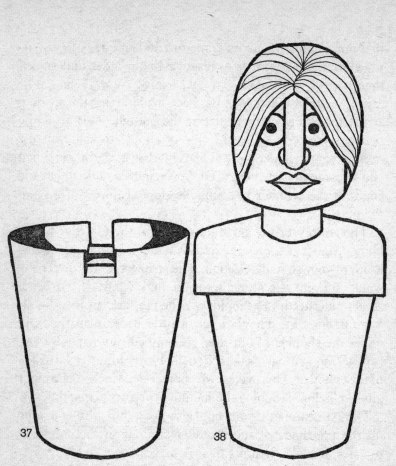

37   38

Look at figure 37. This, again, is a basic cylinder, though it has some slight differences. To begin with, it is larger than any of the cylinders you have made so far (after all, a body is bigger than a head). The top of the body cylinder should still be small enough to fit under the shoulder section, so that none of it sticks out, but so that the shoulders can fit neatly over the top of it.

The top of the body has to be squeezed and distorted slightly to do this; but it's better to make the cylinder top too narrow than too big as, when you come to add clothing, you can always use these additions to disguise the cylinder underneath them.

The cylinder in figure 37 has been made so that the opening at the top is bigger than that at the bottom. This gives the body a 'waisted' look, and is very simple to achieve: just overlap your cylinder more at one end than at the other. When you become more experienced, you might be able to cut the edges of the cylinder to a suitable slope, before you overlap them.

The reason for the small tabs cut into the top edge of the body cylinder becomes apparent when you look at the underneath of your shoulder section. The strip across the underside would prevent the straight top of the cylinder from being stuck underneath the shoulders. The tabs are cut in as an allowance for this. They are cut a little wider than the strip under the shoulders; but they are only cut in to about 2 cm. (1 in.). Don't cut across the tab; bend it over towards the inside of the cylinder. This makes two 'brackets', which you can put glue on, before dropping the shoulders in place across the tabs.

For extra strength, you could also put a thin coating of glue on the underside of the shoulder section, so that where it touches, it sticks (figure 38).

Figure 39 shows a body shape, attached to the shoulders, and with the first layers of folds across it. To make these folds, take a piece of rectangular card of suitable size, with the grain running from side to side. Into this, cut a number of smooth curves, as shown in figure 40. The two corner pieces are not needed, they are too short to use for a draped effect, though they might be useful for some other part of the cosume. Put a dab of glue under the top end of the first section, and stick this to one of the shoulders. Note that the top of each curve is

very slightly narrower than the bottom.

Wait a bit for the glue to dry slightly, and then curve the piece over and join it to the waist. It doesn't matter if the piece is too long; it can still be joined at waist level.

By putting glue only at the ends of the strips, you should be able to make the shape of the folds independent of the shape of the body cylinder. Stick the next strip in almost the same

41   42

place as the first on the shoulder, but sloped so that the bottom
overlap is not as close. You should have more of the first strip
showing at the waist than at the shoulder; except the last
strip, of course, which shows just as you cut it.

If you have any strips left over, you could make a similar
draped effect across this set of curves, from the other shoulder.
It is more important that you end up with a regular, even
effect than that you use all the shapes you cut.

If you keep the curves regular across the whole body, each
curve complementing the last, the card will end up looking
similar to a draped fabric. If you experiment, there are several
curves which could be cut into the card as a basic drape.
You could even use the straight-strip method described in the
next chapter, once you have mastered it.

43   44

In figures 41 to 44 you can see a few ideas for dressing the
bodies, and adding character to faces.

The groom (figure 41) has the addition of a moustache,
which is a simple shape to cut out; and even simpler if you
remember to fold the piece you are cutting in half first, so
that you cut out both sides together. The carnation in his lapel
is made of a number of layers, each one smaller than the last,
and each with small points cut all the way round. These are
then 'fluffed out' to give an irregular effect. His tie is made of
a coloured strip, which has stripes of another colour glued on
to it. The lapels of his jacket are made like two curved strips,
but with the shaping added as they are cut, again two at a
time, by folding the paper.

If you intend to give your character a close-fitting garment, it is easiest to cut your basic body and shoulder shapes in the colour you intend using.

The bride (figure 42) has the front of her dress made in this way, the lapels this time being left as smooth curves. Her headdress is stuck to the top of her hair shape with tabs, after the hair, of curved strips, is complete. The curls in the headdress are made as ringlet curls, and are stuck in afterwards. The bride's eyebrows can be cut from very fine strips of black paper (or you can cheat, and use a fibre pen, if you find this too difficult).

The witch (figure 43) has a gown which uses the curved strips as shown earlier, and the conical hat with hair under it. She has also been made to look older by placing small curved pieces of paper, in layers, under her eyes.* The eyelids can be pushed out from the inside of the cylinder, as suggested for the chin shape, and the white eye strip inserted afterwards. If you make eyelids, it is also possible to cut out and add very fine eyelashes. The witch also has the addition of a mole on her chin, which is a small circle cut from a darker colour.

The woman in figure 44 has cheeks, which make use of the offcuts from making her nose (complex method). The cheeks are simply made from the piece of the nose which was folded over. This is turned upside-down, so that it is a mirror image of the nose shape, and the top edge is cut into a curve, to fit in with the eye shape. The folded part of this section is then slipped behind the nose and stuck there. The cheeks will fall on each side of the mouth, and these can be pulled slightly apart before sticking, which will also help give them some

*You might like to note at this point, that this sort of curved strip can also be used as eyelids, if you make your eye shapes according to the complex method (p. 17).

shape. Her 'bun' of hair is made separately, and is stuck on after her basic hairstyle has been completed, in the same way as the bride's headdress and hair. Her collar is made from paper doyleys (see Chapter 8).

Chapter 7

Before moving on to fixing arms and legs to the body cylinder, there is one technique which is useful to learn. If you try it later, the arms will get in the way – and by using it you will find that legs are not always necessary.

It is the full, long dress. This is quite a simple operation, and very effective. It makes a good stand for your figure; and it involves a technique which is not altogether new to you – the overlapping of strips of paper.

When you have fixed the body on to the head and shoulders of your model, cut a large number of long strips, with the grain running across the narrow width. (These strips should be 1 cm. to 2 cm. [$\frac{1}{2}$–1 in.] wide.)

If you look at figure 45, you will see that the first part of this operation takes place with the body section upside-down. Each of your long strips has to be stuck by one end to the waist of the body. You will possibly find it easier to glue each strip-end before you attach it, rather than putting a band of glue round the waistline, as this will dry out before you have gone all the way round. It may be necessary to go round with a second, and possibly even a third, layer so that when the body is turned up the right way, the strips fall into a natural shape, without any gaps between them. It is essential to use layers, as there will probably be gaps towards the base of the shape where the strips fall wider apart.

45

46

If you can put your model on a milk-bottle, or something similar, you will be able to see where the strips fall naturally (figure 46). Where they overlap one another, they can be stuck together. If two strips are side by side, but do not overlap, they can be stuck by gluing a strip across behind them. This sticking has to be done all the way round the bell shape. If there are any gaps in it when you have all possible strips glued together, the holes can be filled in from the inside of the shape with any left-over pieces of the same colour; but make sure that the glue doesn't show.

Don't flatten the curve of the dress out at the waist. The idea of this method is to get a 'ballooning' effect for the skirt at the waist. If you want to make a straight dress, you can use the same method, but without turning your model upside-down in the first step.

This technique of overlaid strips can also be used for full sleeves, or blouses, and to make a body look fat and full – as long as you are careful, in these cases, to make strips that look 'natural' and like folds in the material.

To finish off the dress, and give your model a stand, the bottom overlaps of the strips can be trimmed off to a point where you think the dress should end. Keep testing the model's balance as you do this, as it will only stand up if the bottom edge is straight enough.

The technique for making arms is the same as that for making legs, as these are very similar shaped limbs. You should be able to judge from the size of the body you have made how wide the cylinders for arms and legs should be. These cylinders have to be much longer than any you have made so far, and possibly narrower. The sloping sections (figure 47) can be cut into the cylinder by a simple method which, provided it is done with sharp scissors, won't damage the shape too much.

Put the *whole* cylinder, when you have made it, between the scissor blades, and cut off a section at an angle (as shown by the dotted line in figure 47 – this fits on to the shoulder). This is just the same as cutting out the two pieces at once – only this time, it's 'in the round'. You will be able to round off the sharp points of this slope to a smoother curve by trimming it afterwards.

46

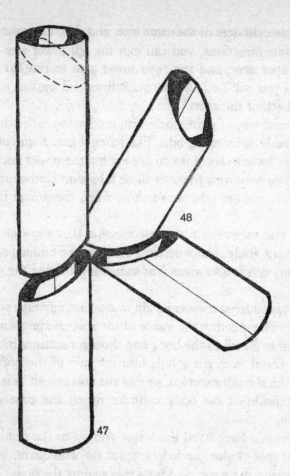

48

47

At about the waist level, or slightly higher, cut another sloped line through the cylinder. This slope allows you to give the arm a bend at the elbow. The remainder of the cylinder can be turned round the other way (figure 48) before you join the two sections together again.

You will notice that the seam line is now turned towards you. This is the only seam line to be seen so far; but if you make *two* cylinders of the same size, and then cut your slopes in *opposite* directions, you can join the *left* lower arm to the *right* upper arm; and the *right* lower arm to the *left* upper . . . and you will find all your seam lines end up out of sight at the back of the arms.

The best way of fixing these arm sections to each other and to the body is by using tabs, like fixing a hat. Some of these tabs may have to show if you are joining the upper and lower arms. You may wish to cover these tabs with clothes anyway, in which case the tabs won't show when the model is completed.

The arm tubes must be made whether they show or not. It gives you a guide as to where the arms will be under a piece of clothing; and it also gives you something to glue the clothes to.

The shoulder section can help to disguise any tabs you use. They can be glued to the inside of the arm opening, and then bent out to attach to the body and shoulder sections invisibly.

You could even cut a hole into the side of the body, just under the shoulder section, so that the arm can sit in it, glued to the inside of the body cylinder round the edge of this opening.

When you have fixed the lower arm on to the upper arm, another spot of glue can help support the whole arm. You can glue behind the wrist, and hold this against the body; or you can glue any part of the arm which is close enough against the body to be stuck.

If you have to put clothes on the body or arm sections, it would be wise to leave the gluing of the arm until the clothes are on, and stick it then.

If you want to give your model extra support, stick it as it is so far on to a piece of backing board, which should be slightly stiffer. This gives you extra support to build up from, as well as supplying your character with something to stand against.

The same instructions for fixing the arms apply to attaching the legs to the body, except that when the upper leg is fixed the method is much more simple. The bottom of the body cylinder is already open, and the top of the leg section just needs a band of glue round it before it is pressed to the sides of the body cylinder. As the top of the leg is hidden, there is

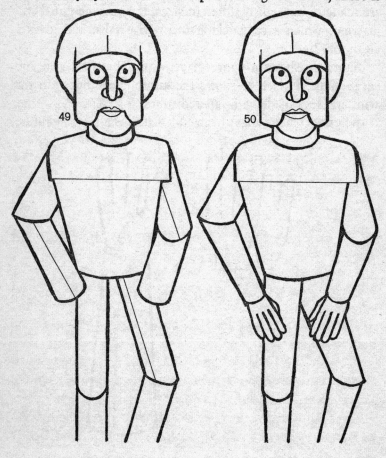

no need to cut a slope on it. The angle of the leg depends on the angle at which it is stuck inside the body.

If you want to do arms without clothing, or legs which show, these shapes will have to be tapered so that the arm can be wide at the shoulder and narrower at the wrist; and the leg shape can taper down to the ankle.

In this way, you will also be able to design your cylinders more carefully so that they can fit into one another. If they are made to be slightly different sizes, they can be glued and inserted, which saves sticking them with tabs, and gives a clean join line.

Figure 49 shows a figure made with cylindrical arm and leg sections. Figure 50 shows the same figure, but with the arms and legs made with tapered tubes.

In figure 50 hands have been added at the ends of the tubes.

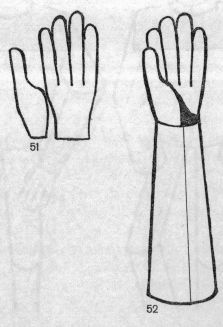

51

52

If you look at figures 51 and 52, you will see that the roundness of the hand shape is obtained by using the cylinder end as a base to put the hand parts on.

The thumb is cut out separately and the four fingers cut out from another section. These are made so that they fit into the open end of the cylinder; if your cylinder opening is too narrow at the wrist, you can either cut it across further along, or, if that makes the arm too short, cut a slanting section (which always makes a wider opening).

Cut the hand out so that the grain runs down the fingers, so that it can curve more easily with your arm cylinder. The fingers are inserted into the cylinder, and glued to the inside edge. (Put the glue on to the hand section. It's too difficult to put it inside the cylinder opening.) Put a pencil or some other solid object in, to help you pinch this section against the sides of the cylinder while the glue dries.

When it is dry, glue the thumb to the cylinder in the same way, but, as shown, against the opposite side, so that the whole hand becomes a continuation of the cylinder, and not a flat object stuck on to the end of it.

When both hand sections have dried, it is possible to bend the fingers inwards. Look at your own fingers to see where the bends should be. Be careful not to get too many creases. Remember that these bends are against the grain, and will show permanently wherever you put them.

Figure 53 shows the basic shape for a foot. The inside curve on this shape should be very slightly larger than the bottom of the leg cylinder, and the two side strips are made longer than necessary, to wrap round the ankle. These can be cut off as the foot is fitted on.

The grain of the paper should run down the length of the foot. The procedure is to wrap the two projecting strips

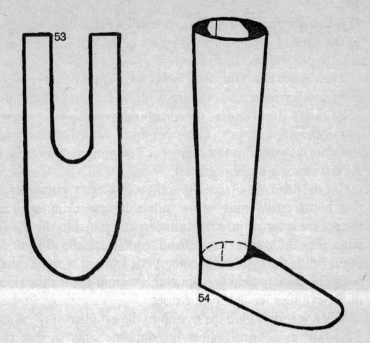

round the bottom of the cylinder, gluing the underside, and cutting them to size. The overlap at the heel should be only very slight (figure 54).

If you position the foot carefully, you can disguise the bottom of the cylinder completely, having the two strips as an ankle section, and the long, rounded section as a toe.

You can add details on to this shape, such as a large flap for a tongue to the shoe; or silver-paper buckles.

Chapter 8

As you now have a full, doll-like figure, either with arms and legs, hands and feet, or with a full-length dress, you can now go on to choose the effects and colours you want to use with the costume, using the various different techniques you know already from making the parts of your figure so far.

In adding things to your character, it's worth remembering that you can make a very slight curve (as in the shoulders) by cutting a line into paper and overlapping the two sections this makes.

That you can cut and overlap curved strips, or straight strips.

That you can stick one colour to another, or combine one coloured section with another, to make a costume more interesting.

It's also worth considering the fact that you can combine one technique with another, for more interesting effects. For instance, if you want to make a full-length dress more interesting, you could use a series of tapered tubes, made to roughly the same length as the arm or leg shape before these are separated into upper and lower parts. Figures 55 and 56 show how you can make two cylinders, side by side, with one long rectangle of card. This also applies to tubes which taper. The extra card is bent back and stuck to the back of the first cylinder.

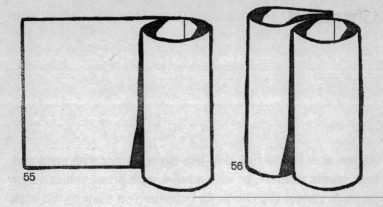

55

56

If you make a few of these, some left as in figure 55, you can join them together side by side, and then insert this piece under the waist of your character. The tops of the cylinders can be squashed a little as you do this, to enable them to stick more firmly.

The join line can be disguised either with an overskirt made of straight strips, or with a broad belt (see plates 2c and 4 of the Jester and the Princess).

If you have found it difficult to cut out the minute circles of card used for the pupils of the eyes, or if you want to make a string of paper pearls, or buttons for a costume, see if you can get hold of a perforator, which is a simple machine for making small holes in paper. The small circles which it cuts out are collected in the base of the machine, and it is these small circles we are interested in. Black-paper offcuts are perfect for eye pupils, while white ones are very useful for necklaces.

These have to be stuck on one at a time. You can use silver card (cream cakes often come in rather nice, useful, gold or silver boxes) to make costume decorations such as brooches or buttons, but you may have trouble sticking some silver or gold papers as the finish tends to come off some of them when you put glue on, and sometimes the glue manages to dull a surface right through from the other side of a piece of card.

If one side of the card is plain white, then the gluing process will be easier. This sort of card can be used for cutting out crowns, buckles and other ornaments.

Another useful thing for decoration is a paper doyley. This is such an effective technique, however, that it's quite easy to get carried away once you start using it, and you could end up with a figure covered with doyleys, but with very little invention behind the costume design. It's probably better to limit yourself to using only one doyley.

An idea for a collar is shown in Chapter 6, but doyleys can also be used as trimming on aprons or dresses. The Jester is holding a handkerchief made from a small piece of doyley (see plate 2c).

The effect of fur is created with the use of tissue paper, which can also be used as a petticoat, or even for a feather boa.

To get the tissue to give the nice, crumpled effect, you will first have to screw a whole sheet of it into a tight ball. Open this ball out again, and *tear* it into small pieces. These should be rough shapes of about 3 cm. (1 in.). When you have all your tissue in pieces of this size, crumple a piece again (this way, you get more creases on it), and place it where you want it to go. Allow this first piece time to dry. It is the basic anchor piece. When it is dry, crumple another piece and glue it, and press this tightly against the first piece; then you can add the other pieces in quick succession, until the area you want to cover is completed.

If you are making a petticoat, the tissue can be stuck round the underneath edge of a skirt. The next time round, you can stick tissue to tissue and so on to the centre, building up a strong tissue layer, in the same way as you reached the middle of the head with the glued–together ringlet curls.

Chapter 9

Cutting a line into a piece of paper, and then gluing together the overlapping pieces of the cut, will give the paper a slope. This is also the basis of making a cone.

A further device using this cutting and gluing technique is the *double curve*, which will allow the paper to be curved in two directions at once. Figure 57 shows how such a piece can be cut so that it produces an overlap on two edges. Overlap and glue these sections so that they are the same: this will force your paper round in a slightly rounded shape. This is very similar to a second cut in the shoulder shape; and the grain of the paper runs in the same way, from side to side.

Plate 6a takes this idea even further. Several lines are cut into the shape (which is square in this instance) and then these lines are glued and stuck, each one overlapping the other to about half the width. This helps create a smoother line to the curve, as it is really a series of straight edges. This means that the closer they are together, the smoother the curve will be.

A tab is put underneath the shape to hold the semi-cylinder in place. In many cases it doesn't matter whether this tab is hooked to the inside or to the outside of the shape, as often (when making the hedgehog, for instance) the whole piece is covered with another layer.

For the face, a semi-circle cone has been added, stuck under

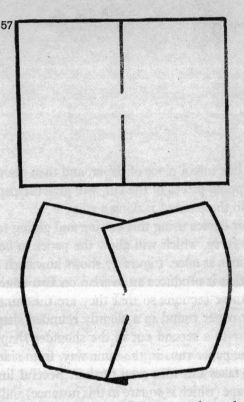

the end of the body section; and that completes the hedgehog framework.

You will gradually learn how to 'undress' a shape, so that you can work out which shapes are needed to make a basic framework for your own finished pieces.

The simple – yet effective – process for finishing off the hedgehog is to lay on his coat of prickles. Cut out some 'comb' strips, as you did for making hair; but this time the strips are made both thinner and shorter than before. As you want a prickly effect, you could even cut these *across* the grain, instead of *with* it.

The single caution about putting these strips on to the body is that you should think about which direction the prickles should go. If you have ever seen a rolled-up hedgehog, you will have seen all the prickles lying over one another, towards the tail end. This means that the bottom layer is at the tail end; and the top layer, therefore, is at the head end, and should be put on *last*. So start putting the combed strips on at the tail end.

Lay on the first strip of prickles. Lay the second strip over this, as shown, so that it covers half the first strip; and then the third strip, and so on, all over the body.

Don't cover the face with spikes – hedgehogs have fairly smooth faces. Its eyes are put on either before or after the spikes, in just the same way as on a face cylinder; and you could even cut into the cone to give the hedgehog a small mouth.

The sheep and pig (plate 6b) have been made by using exactly the same basic curve for their backs, but they have had legs added, at the four pointed edges on the curve shape.

The sheep has a layer of finger curls all over its body, again, starting at the tail end, and its face is cut into to make a double curve on the nose end.

The pig has a curly tail, made by cutting a spiral in a piece of pink paper, and then pulling it out and gluing it to the body at various points – and its nose is stuck on with tabs across a basic tapering cylinder.

The ears, in both cases, have been stuck on by folding a strip over at one end.

Of course, a pig can't have a coat of paper strips, so the basic shape is seen, and the tab has to be underneath.

Chapter 10

Look at figure 58. It shows half a cat. Why half a cat? Because the paper has been folded in two, and this, as you know, means that you can cut out two pieces of the same shape and size at the same time. This cat has been made so that its centre falls in the same place as the fold line and, by cutting where shown, a lot of the folded edge is still joined together after the cat has been opened out. This makes both halves the same, and adds up to a *symmetrical* cat.

In plate 7a you will see a flower in a flowerpot, a bird, a clown and another cat. They are all symmetrical and have been cut out by this same method.

Try looking for a symmetrical shape for yourself; or try cutting out the cat shape. Finer lines (such as those showing the cat's legs, or the clown's mouth) can be used, as long as you don't get too complicated and start cutting one shape into another. If you do this, the shapes are likely to fall away, and you could be left with a blank space. Keep as much of the fold as possible, so that when you open out your shape, you have a nice solid piece, with no gaps except the intentional ones!

Pieces like these are better if they are mounted on a piece of backing board.

Before the clown was mounted, some of the fold lines were pinched out so that the fold pointed the other way. His nose is made to stick out from his face, and his shirt-front from his

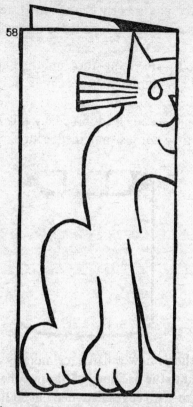

body. This is *low relief* work (i.e. the piece doesn't stand out much from the flat surface of the board). It depends on what you make as to which parts stick out, and which should have backward creases.

As you cut these folded pieces, you can occasionally open out the work, to see where you want to put in any extra details, then fold it together again to put them in. Any of the techniques we've already explored in this book can be used to make low-relief work more varied and interesting. The difference is that you start work with a flat piece of board, and keep your curved pieces fairly close to it. Instead of using full cylinders, use semi-cylinders, pulled to the backing board with tabs.

Take a look at plate 7b, of Alice and the Duchess. None of these pieces sticks out more than 5 cm. (2 in.) from the black background.

All the techniques involved in making this have been dealt with already: they are just modified a little, to make them a bit flatter.

Figure 59 shows how a flatter cylinder is made. The two pieces attached to the backing board can either be stuck on as they curve or the two edges flattened out so that they become 'attached' tabs. This is a quick and easy shape to do. It can also be used to hold a *flat* shape away from the surface, if you stick it to the upper side of this curve.

Another way of holding a flat piece away from the surface is by attaching double tabs behind it, so that the fold on each end can be glued to the backing board. Try to get your tabs the same colour as the backing board, so that they disappear completely. If you have any trouble disguising them, try laying a piece of paper the same colour as the backing over a folded end of the tab.

If you intend doing a piece of low-relief paper sculpture, it's advisable to plan ahead a little, so that you know which pieces you want to be the roundest, and which pieces can be left flat.

The Duchess's headpiece and body are the roundest pieces, but to get these in the right places, the face (which is a low, flat piece) had to be finished first. The chin was not stuck to the backing, but to the rest of the face, so that her costume could be slipped under it as it was made.

When the dress was finished, the legs were put on, and, as with Alice, one of the legs is cut out flat, and glued on to the black card. The other leg is made from a rounded piece of card, and a shoe added to it.

Alice's face, arm and one leg are all cut from flat pieces of card; it is the roundness of the rest of her body which gives the impression of shapes for these, as they are forced into different angles.

Figure 60 shows another shape used in this piece, in the dress and apron folds. It is basically the same as a flat cylinder, but with one end glued on what might be considered the 'wrong' side. This is similar to the 'reverse' cylinder, shown in figure 56.

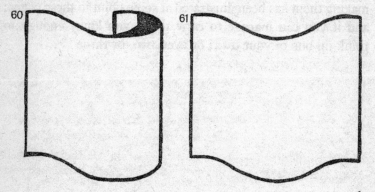

Figure 61 also shows a useful low-relief shape, which again is familiar. This is made by gluing a rectangle down one edge only, waiting for the glue to dry, and then sticking the second, opposite edge so that is slightly closer to the first edge. This makes the centre of the piece lift away from the backing.

Overlapping strips, semi-cylinders, double curves and a great number of other techniques can be used in low-relief work.

As in standard paper sculpture, it's all a matter of working out *where* each technique could fit in to the best effect.

Throughout this book, you have been learning different ways to get different effects, by the different things involved in making paper-sculpture people and animals.

Now it's time to use a few of these methods in making quick and easy things, all involving processes you should be able to recognize.

Some of these 'party pieces' are gathered together in plate 8b. They are not explained; you should be able to recognize how to make them by what you have learned. Each step in making them has been illustrated at some point in these pages; and if you can manage to copy these, you know enough to think up one of your own; or even two, or three . . .